WELCOME TO THE NEIGHBORHOOD
10302

by

Mary-Antonia Lombardi

Copyright © 2022 by Mary-Antonia Lombardi

All rights reserved.

No portion of this book may be reproduced in any form without written permission from the publisher or author, except as permitted by U.S. copyright law.

This publication is designed to provide accurate and authoritative information in regard to the subject matter covered. It is sold with the understanding that neither the author nor the publisher is engaged in rendering legal, investment, accounting or other professional services. While the publisher and author have used their best efforts in preparing this book, they make no representations or warranties with respect to the accuracy or completeness of the contents of this book and specifically disclaim any implied warranties of merchantability or fitness for a particular purpose. No warranty may be created or extended by sales representatives or written sales materials. The advice and strategies contained herein may not be suitable for your situation. You should consult with a professional when appropriate. Neither the publisher nor the author shall be liable for any loss of profit or any other commercial damages, including but not limited to special, incidental, consequential, personal, or other damages.

Book cover by Mary-Antonia Lombardi and John B. Fantini

Illustrations by Mary-Antonia Lombardi

First edition 2022

For Emma,
I love you the most!

And for Pete, my biggest supporter.

And of course, for Vito and Zola who make me giggle.

And lastly, for Rudy and Robo.
You are fur-ever in our hearts.

FUN FACT!

Port Richmond is a neighborhood on the North Shore of Staten Island, one of New York City's 5 boroughs.

WHERE AM I?

This is where I like to come smell the trees and chase birds and squirrels.

It's the town square, called Veterans Park. And across from the park is the library. Mom loves to go there and read all the books they have inside.

FUN FACT!

Veterans Park is Staten Island's oldest and first public park. Originally called Port Richmond Park, it was renamed Veterans Park after World War II as a tribute to the local service members.

Before it was renovated, the Port Richmond branch of the New York Public Library had a secret dwelling. On the top floor, hidden from public view, was a four room apartment. Many years ago, the custodian would live there and take care of the library during the night.

FUN FACT!

In the past, Port Richmond's location on the Kill Van Kull made it a main ferry launch from Staten Island to New Jersey. Ferries ran from there until 1962. Today, the Kill Van Kull serves as an important route for ships that transport goods from all over the world.

The Bayonne Bridge is one of the longest steel arch bridges in the world. You can drive or walk over it.

Phew! I'm putting a lot of miles on these little legs of mine today.

On this corner there used to be a hotel. I heard that a famous person lived there a long time ago.

FUN FACT! Aaron Burr was the third Vice President of the United States under Thomas Jefferson.

ON THIS SITE STOOD THE
ST. JAMES HOTEL
BUILT SHORTLY AFTER
THE AMERICAN REVOLUTION.
AARON BURR DIED HERE
SEPTEMBER 14, 1836

FUN FACT!

This Burial Place has 45 heroes of the wars that created America: The American Revolution, The War of 1812, and The Civil War.

The Graveyard is located on the grounds of a Reform church that was originally built by Dutch settlers in 1680.

BURIAL PLACE OF THE DUTCH SETTLERS OF THE NORTH SHORE UNTIL 1696 AROUND WHICH PORT RICHMOND WAS BUILT.

Grandma told me that this building right here was once a beautiful theater.

She used to call it the "fancy theater" and said she liked it better than all the rest.

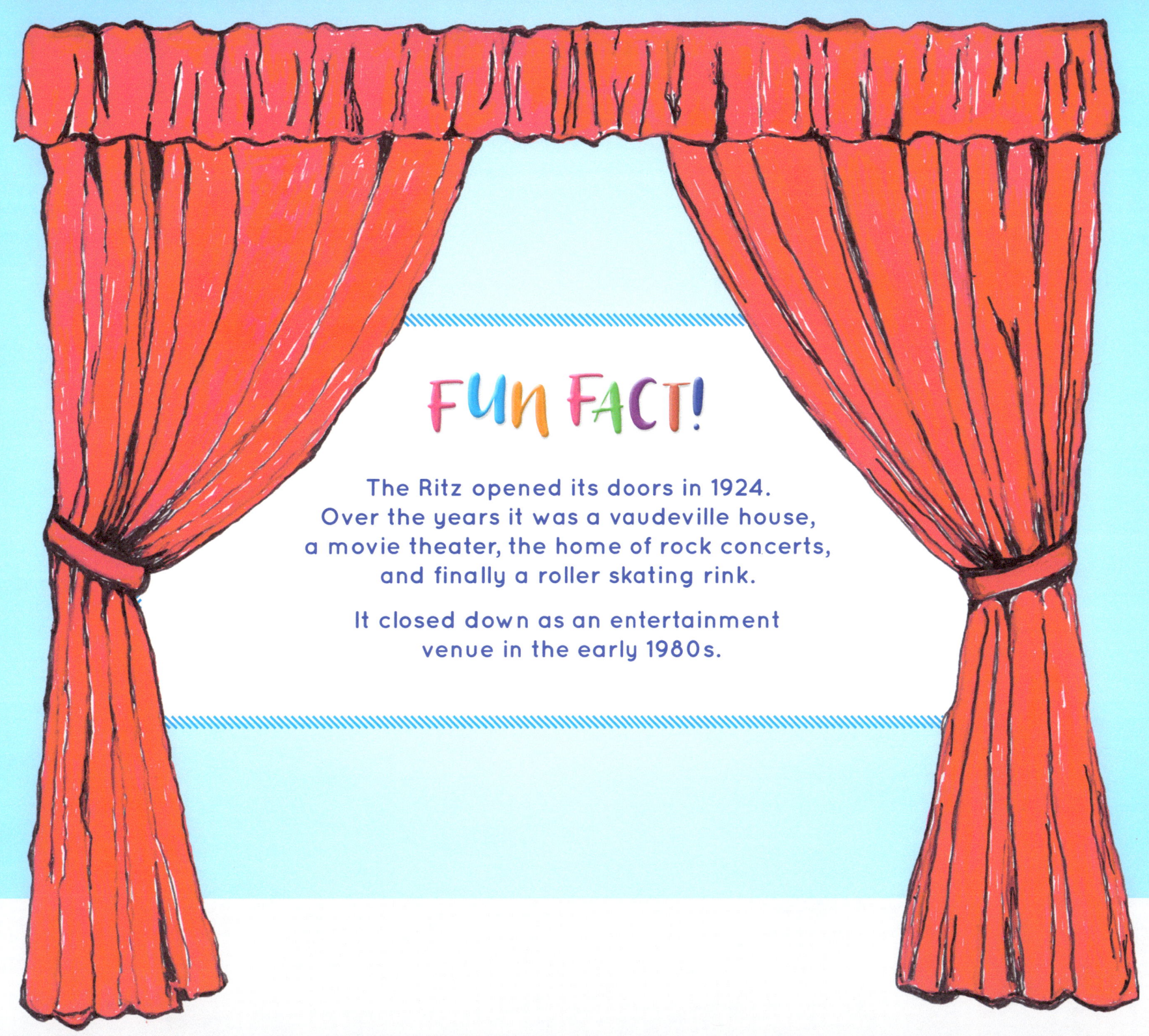

FUN FACT!

The Ritz opened its doors in 1924. Over the years it was a vaudeville house, a movie theater, the home of rock concerts, and finally a roller skating rink.

It closed down as an entertainment venue in the early 1980s.

Before we go home, I want to show you one of my favorite things to do in Port Richmond. I call it, "Going for a slice and an ice."

First we will eat some super yummy pizza from this place called Denino's.

After that, we'll cross the street and get the best Italian ice ever from a place called Ralph's.

We're back home Zola!

Look, big sister is waiting for us.

I sure hope you enjoyed our walk, and I hope it made you feel at ease with your new neighborhood.

Vito is our beloved dog who became part of our family through a local animal rescue in 2012. Although small in stature, he has a big personality and likes to think he is king.

Nine years later, Zola became part of our family, through the same rescue group. She was very shy and timid at first, but with Vito's love and compassion, she soon adapted into her new surroundings.

Thank Yous and Acknowledgments:

Production of this book was partially funded by a DCA Arts Grant from Staten Island Arts, with funding from the New York City Department of Cultural Affairs.

To my friends and family who listened, discussed, gave input and tons of support and encouragement throughout this process.

And a special shout out to John Fantini who planted the seed. You made my vision a reality with your graphic design expertise.

Index

Veterans Park—Bordered by Heberton Avenue, Park Avenue, Bennett Street and Vreeland Street

Port Richmond Branch of The New York Public Library—75 Bennett Street

Bayonne Bridge—Located between Morningstar Road and Newark Avenue

St. James Hotel—Was located on the corner of Port Richmond Avenue and Richmond Terrace

The Dutch Reformed Church and Graveyard—54 Port Richmond Avenue

The Ritz Theater—Was located on Port Richmond Avenue and Anderson Avenue

Denino's Pizzeria and Tavern—524 Port Richmond Avenue

Ralph's Famous Italian Ices—501 Port Richmond Avenue

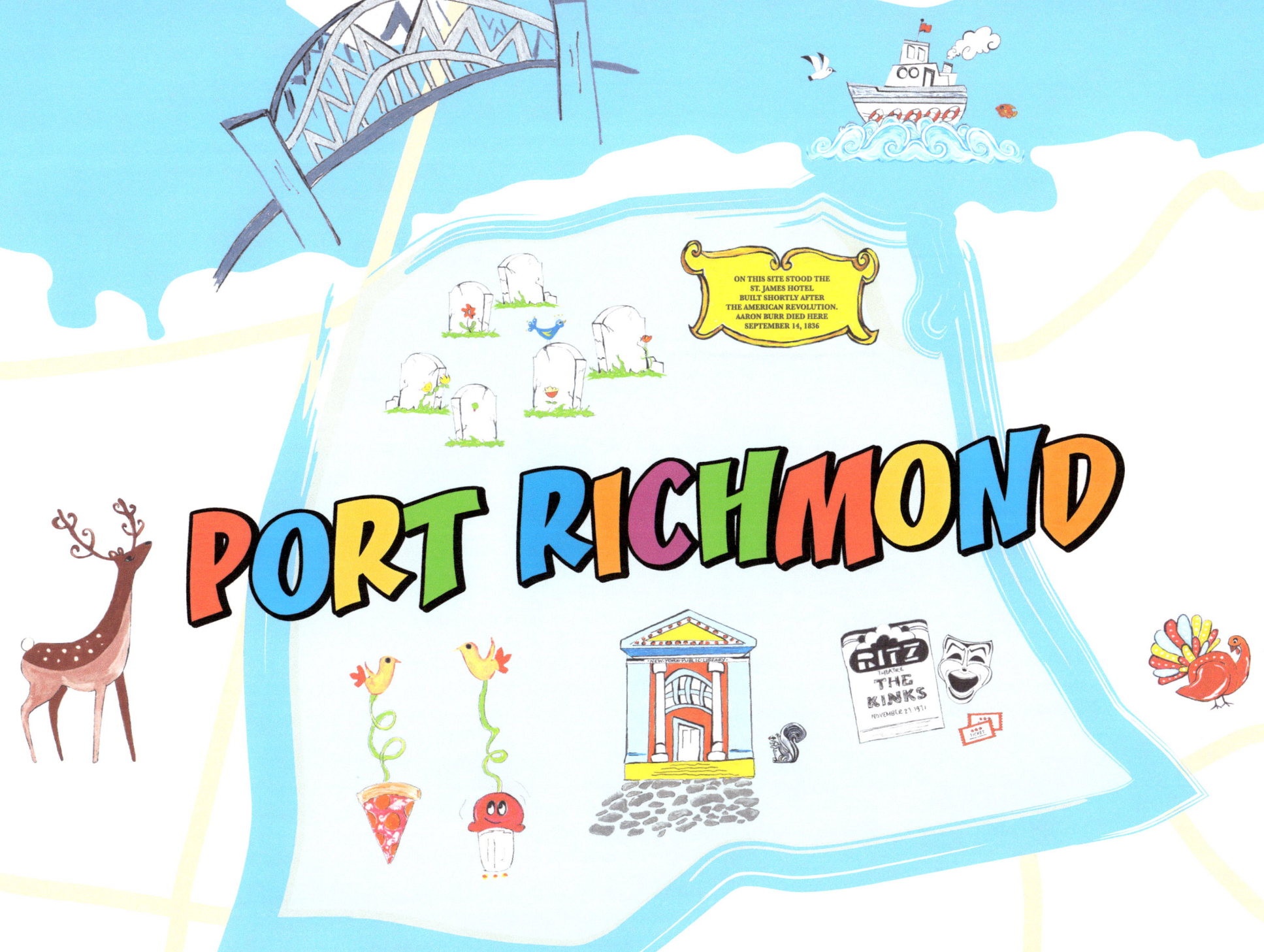